Poland

Flag of Gdańsk

Gdańsk Poland Gdansk Old Port Motlawa River

Poland Gdansk Artus Court Neptunbrunnen

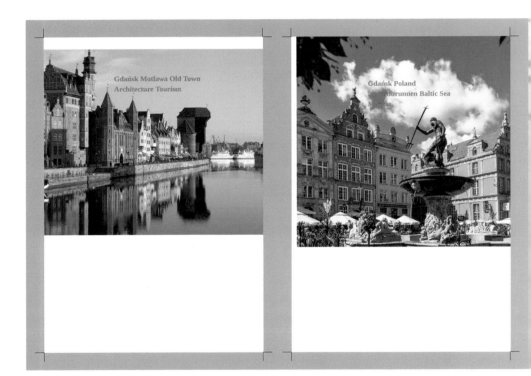

Gdansk Poland Arena Venue Sports Architecture

Gdansk Poland City Cities Urban Apartments Pods

Architecture Poland Gdansk Crane Medieval Old

Building Architecture Facade Sky Clouds Trees

Gdańsk Poland Water Building Polish Architecture

Gdańsk Architecture The Old Town

Nature Baltic Beach Clouds Dusk Evening Gdansk

Sleeping Lion Street Statue Monument Gdansk

Building Poland Gdansk Port City Body Of Water

Gdańsk Building
Ivy

The Seagulls The Pier Sea The Baltic Sea Nature

European Union Europe Travel Poland Map Country

University Medical Centre in Gdańsk

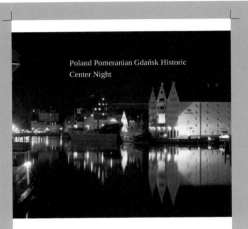

Poland Pomeranian Gdańsk Historic Center Night

Poland Gdansk St Mary's Church

Gdańsk Small Mill Mur Pruski

Gdansk Poland Buildings City Cities Sky Clouds

Gdansk Church Historically Poland

Gdansk Channel View

Ship Black Pearl Sea
Gdańsk

Gdańsk City Vistas Townhouses
Old Town

Nature People Baltic Beach Clouds Couple Deck

Gdańsk City Historically Poland

Aircraft Airport Gdańsk

Gdańsk Night Crane Evening Street The Old Town

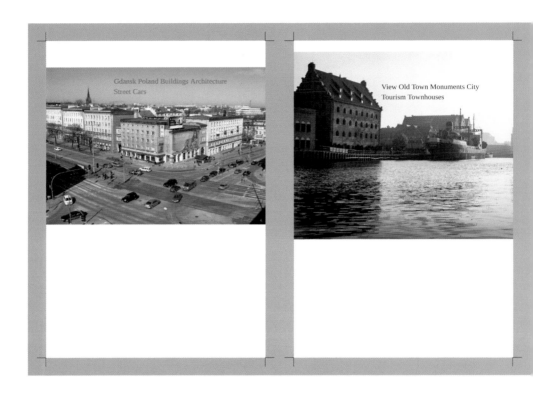

Gdansk Poland Buildings Architecture Street Cars

View Old Town Monuments City Tourism Townhouses

Gdańsk Poland Gdansk

Gdańsk The Old Town Armory Monument Old Houses

Gdańsk Historic Center Cottages Facade Ornament

Gdańsk The Old Town Crane Old Motława Sołdek

The Pier Sea Beach The Baltic Sea Gdańsk Poland

Gdansk Poland Buildings Architecture Building

Gdansk Poland Railroad Railway Buildings City

Gdansk Poland City Wet Damp Weather Rain Trees

Architecture Poland Gdansk Crane Medieval Travel

Gdansk Gdańsk War Memorial Memorial Westerplatte

Architecture Poland Gdansk Docks Port Channel

Gdańsk The Old Port Moltawy Poland

Gdańsk Port The Waterfront Motlawa Poland

Gdansk Danzig Poland Travel City Building

Gdańsk Mur Pruski Motlawa River

Flag Poland The Nation Symbol
Gdańsk The Mast

Gdańsk Poland Aer

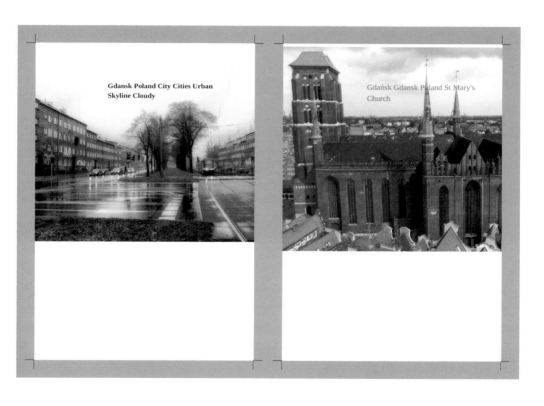

Gdansk Poland City Cities Urban Skyline Cloudy

Gdańsk Gdansk Poland St Mary's Church

Gdansk Bikes Bicycle

Gdansk Poland Travel

View Shipping Water Polo Ship Haven

Gdansk The Old Town Church Old Town Monuments

House Architecture Outdoor Horizontal No Person

Gdańsk The Town Hall Architecture The Cathedral

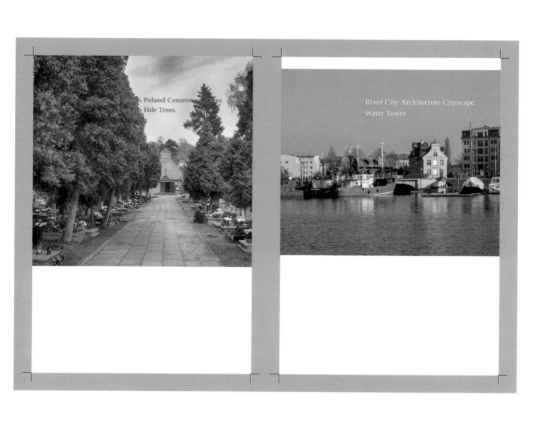

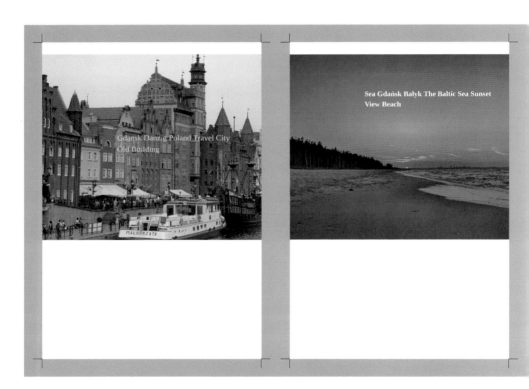

Gdansk Danzig Poland Travel City Old Building

Sea Gdańsk Bałyk The Baltic Sea Sunset View Beach

Gdańsk The Old Town Old Motlawa

View Panorama Architecture Building Drawbridge

Gdańsk Fortress Vistula Mouth The Museum Napoleon

Gdańsk The Old Town Crane Old Motława Townhouses

Gdańsk Kamienica Architecture Old Town
The Old Town

Airport Gdańsk Rębiechowo Wałesa
Port Architecture

River Boat Water City Poland Gdańsk Harbor Blue

Gdańsk The Town Hall The Museum Old Town The Market

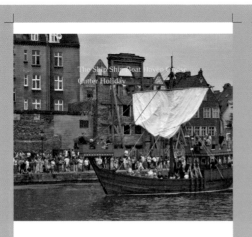

The Ship Ship Boat Haven Cruise Cutter Holiday

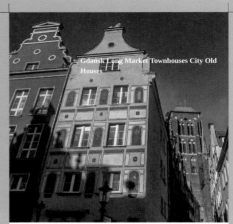

Gdansk Long Market Townhouses City Old Houses

Trojmesto Gdańsk Poland
Architecture Club

Gdańsk Architecture Nightshot
Marketplace

Gdańsk Architecture Old Town The Old Town

Poland Gdańsk City Center History Architecture

Trojmesto Gdańsk Poland
Architecture Cities

Gdańsk Soldiers History

Building Architecture Brick
Gdańsk

Gdansk Long Seashore
Tourists

Ship Shipping Gdańsk The Ship Yacht Sailing

Gdańsk Sołdek Ship Tourism The Old Town

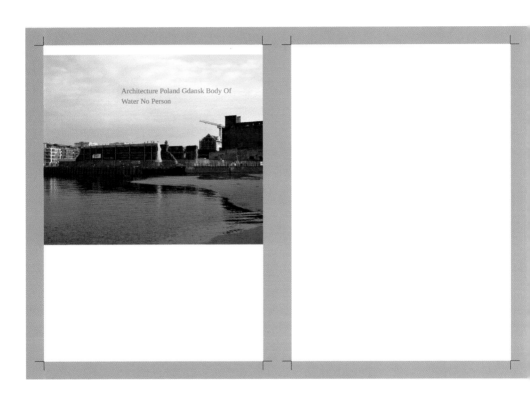
Architecture Poland Gdansk Body Of Water No Person

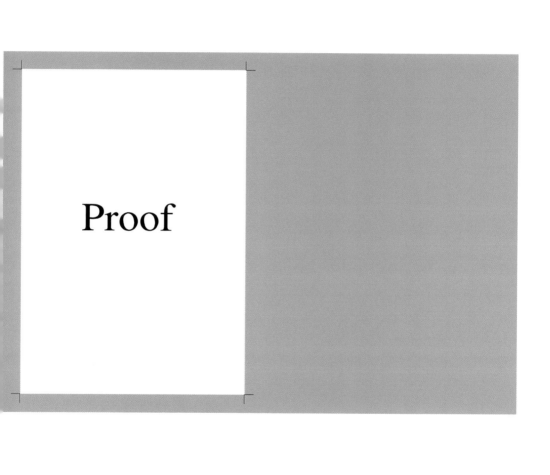
Proof

Printed in Great Britain
by Amazon

33623115R00041